Wicket Wit

summersdale

WICKET WIT

Reprinted 2006 and 2007

Summersdale Publishers Ltd
46 West Street
Chichester
West Sussex
PO19 1RP
UK

www.summersdale.com

Printed and bound in Finland

ISBN: 1-84024-541-7
ISBN: 978-1-84024-541-7

Contents

Editor's note

HRH the Duke of Edinburgh once scoffed at the 'widely held and quite erroneous belief that cricket is just another game'. This eclectic compendium, for its part, ably disproves such misconceptions, showing how the relevance of cricket extends beyond the pitch to literature, society, politics and philosophy. In fact, the gentleman's game has inspired some of the most profound insights and off-the-cuff humour to be found in any collection of quotations.

Amongst these pages there are timeless classics as well as a few more obscure commentaries to raise the eyebrow of even the most dedicated cricket fanatic. From cricketers to commentators, celebrities to politicians, poets to comedians, it seems everyone has something to say about this age-old game. There's banter about the pitfalls of batting and bowling, quirky quips about the nuances of the game and acidic attacks from and on the press. Dip into each section and you are sure to find something to crease you up.

The delightful mix of run-out rebuttals, wicket wisecracks, oval orations and howzat humiliations in this side-splitting book will ensure you'll never be stumped for a return again.

BATTING

David Gower makes
batting look as easy
as drinking tea.

Sir Leonard Hutton

Cricket is a batsman's game. The city of London has never emptied to watch a bowler as it did to watch Bradman.

E. W. Swanton, English cricket writer and commentator (1907–2000)

It's hard work making batting look effortless.

David Gower, English television personality and former cricketer

I couldn't bat for the length of time required to score 500. I'd get bored and fall over.

Denis Compton, English cricketer (1918–1997)

When I was watching Fred Astaire
I used to think, here was a chap who
would have been a great batsman.

Sir Leonard Hutton, English cricketer (1916–1990)

Whenever I saw Wally Hammond
batting, I felt sorry for the ball.

Sir Leonard Hutton

When you win the toss – bat. If you
are in doubt, think about it, then
bat. If you have very big doubts,
consult a colleague – then bat.

W. G. Grace, English cricketer
and doctor (1848–1915)

When I'm batting, I like to
pretend I'm a West Indian.

Darren Gough, English cricketer

They came to see me bat,
not to see you bowl.

W. G. Grace on refusing to leave the crease
having been bowled out by the first ball

He looks like and bats like a
librarian: a prodder, a nudger, with
a virile bottom hand that works the
ball to the on side, and a top hand
for keeping his other glove on.

Mike Selvey, English cricket correspondent and former
cricketer, on Bert Vance's Test debut, *The Guardian*

I never wanted to
make a hundred.
Who wants to make
a hundred anyway?
When I first went in,
my immediate objective
was to hit the ball
to each of the four
corners of the field.
After that, I tried
not to be repetitive.

Lord Learie Constantine, Trinidad-born
batsman and political activist (1901–1971)

BOWLING

I don't want to do
the batsman any
permanent injury, just
to cause him concern
– to hurt him a bit.

Dennis Lillee, former Australian cricketer

You can't buy one of them
at a local superstore – it
takes years and years.

Darren Gough, on a good one-day bowler

I bowl so slow that if after I
have delivered the ball I don't
like the look of it, I can run
after it and bring it back.

**J. M. Barrie, Scottish novelist and
dramatist (1860–1937)**

I try to hit the batsman in the
ribcage when I bowl a purposeful
bouncer, and I want it to hurt so
much that the batsman doesn't
want to face me anymore.

Dennis Lillee

You must treat a cricket
ball like a new bride.

**Micky Stewart, former English cricketer
and England cricket manager**

To be a great fast bowler, you
need a big heart and a big bottom.

**Fred Trueman, English commentator,
author and former cricketer**

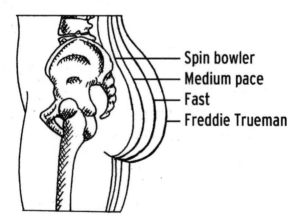

— Spin bowler
— Medium pace
— Fast
— Freddie Trueman

Fast bowling isn't hard
work, it's horse work.

Fred Trueman

I was once timed at 99.97mph,
but that's rubbish, I was
miles faster than that.

Jeff Thompson, former Australian bowler,
reputed to be the fastest ever

His bowling is like shooting down
F-16s with sling shots. Even if they
hit, no damage would be done.

Colin Croft, former West Indies bowler, on
Angus Fraser in the Guyana Test

He bowls like an octopus with piles.

Unknown Australian on former English cricketer
Derek Randall, as reported by Matthew Engel

I don't go as far as that
on my holidays.

Unknown bowler, commenting on the
length of Bob Willis's run-up

There's nothing wrong with
being aggressive – the bloke
down the other end has a bat,
some pads and a helmet.

Simon Jones, Welsh cricketer

Cowans should remember what happened to Graham Dilley, who started out as a genuinely quick bowler. They started stuffing 'line and length' into his ear, and now he has Dennis Lillee's action with Denis Thatcher's pace.

Geoff Boycott, English commentator
and former cricketer

Though essentially good-natured, he had that vital weapon in the fast bowler's armoury, grumpiness.

Simon Hughes, English journalist, author and former cricketer, on Angus Fraser, *A Lot of Hard Yakka*

CELEBRITIES ON CRICKET

I am confident they
play cricket in heaven.
Wouldn't be heaven
otherwise, would it?

Patrick Moore, astronomer

Cricket is basically baseball on Valium.

Robin Williams, American actor and comedian

❧·❧

Is there any sex in it?

Peter Sellers, English comedian and actor
(1925–1980), as a psychiatrist upon first learning
about cricket in *What's New Pussycat?*

❧·❧

Cricket is like sex films. They relieve frustration and tension.

Linda Lovelace, American actress
and star of *Deep Throat*

❧·❧

Cricket is the only game where you can actually put on weight while playing.

Tommy Docherty, former Scottish footballer

It's a funny kind of month,
October. For the really keen
cricket fan, it's when you realise
that your wife left you in May.

**Denis Norden, English comedy writer
and television presenter**

❦

Nothing yet devised by man is
worse for a sick hangover than a
day's cricket in the summer sun.

**Michael Parkinson, English journalist
and television presenter**

It would be extremely difficult for me to choose between singing Elvis Presley songs and scoring a century for England, but I think I would choose a century for England.

Tim Rice, English lyricist, radio presenter and author

———•———

I want to play cricket, it doesn't seem to matter if you win or lose.

Meat Loaf, American singer

———•———

Are you aware, Sir, that the last time I saw anything like that on a top lip, the whole herd had to be destroyed?

Eric Morecambe, English comedian (1926–1984) to the moustached Dennis Lillee

When's the game itself
going to begin?

Groucho Marx, American comedian and actor (1890–
1977), whilst watching a cricket match at Lord's

—◆—

Cricket needs brightening up a bit.
My solution is to let players drink at
the beginning of the game, not after.
It always works in our picnic matches.

Paul Hogan, Australian actor and comedian

—◆—

I find it beautiful to watch
and I like that they break for
tea. That is very cool.

Jim Jarmusch, American film director

There is a widely held and
quite erroneous belief that
cricket is just another game.

HRH The Duke of Edinburgh

It's been a reasonable day
for us boozers up here in the
private boxes, but what about
the geezers queuing and those
blokes munching their sandwiches
up there at the Nursery End?

**Mick Jagger, English rock musician, after
play was abandoned in the Centenary Test
between England and Australia at Lord's**

I suppose doing a love scene with
Raquel Welch roughly corresponds
to scoring a century before lunch.

Oliver Reed, English actor (1938–1999)

I have often thought
how much better a life
I would have had, what
a better man I would
have been, how much
healthier an existence
I would have led, if I
had been a cricketer
instead of an actor.

Sir Laurence Olivier, English actor (1907–1989)

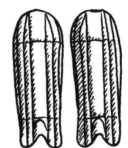

CHARACTER IN CRICKET

Concentration is
sometimes mistaken
for grumpiness.

Michael Atherton, English journalist
and former cricketer

Indomitable; there can be no other epithet to sum up the cricketing spirit in that small and fragile frame.

Denis Mackail, English writer (1892–1971), on J. M. Barrie, *Barrie: The Story of J. M. B.*

If something is not done to excess, it's hardly worth doing.

Peter Roebuck, commenting on Ian Botham's character

It seems that neutral umpires were not used until about 1836 and, hitherto, provided the umpire was a gentleman of good repute, no objection would be taken to his having placed a bet on his team. It would be a point of honour with him to carry out his duties impartially.

Gordon Ross, English cricket journalist (1918–1985), *The Cricketer*

Hambledon is a place that I have a strong dislike to – on account of its morals and dissipation.

Gilbert White, English naturalist and ornithologist (1720–1793), in a letter to his brother Revd John White, on Hambledon, which at the time was one of the centres of cricket

The modern cricketer is not an ogre, nor is he deliberately obstructive. Although in most cases it would be unfair to dismiss him as a spoiled brat, he is too often lazy, ill-disciplined and reluctant to put in the effort and dedication commensurate with the wages he is earning. He has a very low boredom threshold with a constant need to be told what to do with his time.

Bob Willis, English writer, commentator, former cricketer and captain, *Lasting the Pace*

If I had to put it into one word? Integrity.

Sir Donald Bradman, Australian cricketer (1908–2001), on how he wanted to be remembered

---

I regret that my mouth overtakes my brain.

Dermot Reeve, former English cricketer and Somerset coach

I passed him [Cowdrey] and Bailey as they went in on Friday morning. I murmured 'Good Luck'. Cowdrey said 'Thank you, sir'; Bailey said nothing. In five balls Bailey was out and in five hours Cowdrey had made 152. The god of cricket likes good manners.

George Lyttelton, English teacher and essayist (1883–1962), *The Lyttelton Hart-Davis Letters*

COACHES AND CAPTAINS

Have nothing to do with coaches. In fact, if you should see one coming, go and hide behind the pavilion until he goes away.

Bill O'Reilly, Australian cricketer (1905–1992)

Professional coaching is a man trying
to get your legs close together
when other men had spent a lifetime
trying to get them wider apart.

**Rachael Heyhoe-Flint, English cricket journalist
and former captain of the English Ladies XI**

If I had my way, I would take him
to Traitor's Gate and personally
hang, draw and quarter him.

**Ian Botham, English commentator, television
personality and former cricketer, on Ray Illingworth**

I was never coached. I was
never told how to hold a bat.

Sir Donald Bradman

Pray God no professional
may ever captain England.

Lord Hawke, English batsman (1860–1938)

Amateurs have always made,
and always will make, the best
captains, and this is only natural.

Allan Gibson Steel, English cricketer (1858–1914)

Captaincy is 90 per cent luck
and 10 per cent skill. But don't
try it without that 10 per cent.

Richie Benaud, Australian commentator
and former cricketer

Playing against a team with Ian Chappell as captain turns a cricket match into gang warfare.

Mike Brearley, English cricket journalist
and former England captain

You'll have the most miserable time of your life.

Brian Close, former English cricketer,
to Ian Botham on captaincy

COMMENTATOR
CLASSICS

This bowler's like
my dog: three short
legs and balls that
swing each way.

Brian Johnston, English cricket
commentator (1912–1994)

Welcome to Worcester where we have just seen Barry Richards hit one of Basil D'Oliveira's balls clean out of the ground.

Brian Johnston

Neil Harvey's at slip, with his legs wide apart, waiting for a tickle.

Brian Johnston

Turner looks a bit shaky and unsteady, but I think he's going to bat on – one ball left.

Brian Johnston

Fred Titmus has two short
legs, one of them square.

Brian Johnston

Welcome to Leicester, where the
captain Ray Illingworth has just
relieved himself at the Pavilion End.

Brian Johnston

Matthew Fleming used to be in the Green Jackets, but the way he's batting suggests he'd be better suited in the Light Brigade.

Charles Colville, sports commentator, on the Kent batsman giving Lancashire's Ian Austin the charge

It's been a very slow and dull day, but it hasn't been boring. It's been a good, entertaining day's cricket.

Tony Benneworth, Australian cricket commentator

The Queen's Park Oval, exactly as the name suggests, absolutely round.

Tony Crozier, West Indian cricket commentator

England have nothing to lose here, apart from this Test match.

**David Lloyd, English commentator
and former cricketer**

❦

A very small crowd here today. I can count the people on one hand. Can't be more than 30.

**Michael Abrahamson, South African
cricket commentator**

❦

Yorkshire all out 232, Hutton ill – I'm sorry, Hutton 111.

**John Snagge, English newsreader
and commentator (1904–1996)**

I've never got to the bottom of streaking.

**Jonathan Agnew, English cricket
commentator and former batsman**

❧

His throw went absolutely nowhere near where it was going.

Richie Benaud

❧

He's usually a good puller – but he couldn't get it up that time.

Richie Benaud

❧

The slow motion replay doesn't show how fast that delivery was.

Richie Benaud

Those who run cricket in this country, especially at the domestic level, are for the most part a self-serving, pusillanimous and self-important bunch of myopic dinosaurs unable to take any but the shortest-term view of anything.

Henry Blofeld, English cricket commentator

In the rear, the small diminutive figure of Shoaib Mohammed, who can't be much taller or shorter than he is. It's a catch he would have caught 99 times out of a 1000.

Henry Blofeld

It was an excellent performance in the field marred only when Harris dropped Crapp in the outfield.

BBC commentator on a missed chance off
Australian batsman Lindsay Crapp

There was a slight interruption there for athletics.

Richie Benaud on an invading streaker

Laird has been brought in to stand in the corner of the circle.

Richie Benaud

If you go in with two fast bowlers and one breaks down, you're left two short.

Bob Massie, Australian radio commentator and former cricketer

---

Here comes Cunis – his bowling, like his name, neither one thing nor the other.

BBC commentator on Bob Cunis

CRICKET AND SOCIETY

Cricket – it's more
than a game. It's
an institution.

Thomas Hughes, English lawyer and author
(1822–1896), *Tom Brown's Schooldays*

Cricket brings the most opposite characters and the most diverse lives together. Anything that puts very many different kinds of people on a common ground must promote sympathy and kindly feelings.

Kumar Ranjitsinhji, Indian cricketer (1872–1933)

It is more than a game this cricket, it somehow holds up a mirror to English society.

Neville Cardus, English journalist (1889–1975)

The very word 'cricket' has become a synonym for all that is true and honest. To say 'that is not cricket' implies something underhand, something not in keeping with the best ideals.

Sir Pelham Warner, English cricketer (1873–1963)

As every soldier has the baton of a field marshal in his knapsack, so every player has the bat of Lillywhite in his portmanteau.

Almanack, 1868

Cricket is peculiarly a Christian game. No pagan nation has ever played it.

Melbourne newspaper

Oh, I am so glad that you have begun to take an interest in cricket. It is simply a social necessity in England.

P. G. Wodehouse, English author (1881–1975), *Piccadilly Jim*

Cricket, like the upper classes and standards in general, is in permanent decline.

Alan Ross, English poet and editor (1922–2001)

We are nostalgic for the game's past, as well as our own. Some day, I suppose some will look fondly back on boozy, can-rattling spectators, players' rude and self-congratulatory gestures, shirts proper to squash net cricket, helmets less appropriate to Lord's than to Squires Gate.

Roy Fuller, English writer and poet (1912–1991), *From Sparrow Park to Stanley Park*

Innovations invariably are suspect and in no quarter more so than the cricket world.

Gilbert Jessop, English cricketer (1874–1955)

If you made him prime minister tomorrow, he'd pick this country up in ten minutes.

Billy Alley, Australian umpire and former cricketer (1919–2004), on Ian Botham

If Botham is an English folk hero, then this must be an alarming time for the nation.

David Miller, English sports journalist

Cricket's greatness lies in the ability of players to honour a foe. It's the way life should be lived.

Professor William Barclay, Scottish author and theologian (1907–1978)

CRICKET BATS
AT DAWN:
FIGHTING WORDS

Stuff that stiff upper lip crap. Let's see how stiff it is when it's split.

Jeff Thompson

Fred Trueman is bowling. The batsman edges and the ball goes to first slip, and right between Raman Subba Row's legs. At the end of the over, Row ambles past Trueman and apologises.

Row: I should've kept my legs together, Fred.
Trueman: Not you, son. Your mother should've!

So how's your wife, and my kids?

Rod Marsh, former Australian cricketer, to Ian Botham during a match from behind the stumps

---

As Daryll Cullinan was on his way to the wicket, Shane Warne told him he had been waiting 2 years for another chance to humiliate him.

Cullinan: Looks like you spent it all eating.

I know why he's bought a house
by the sea... so he'll be able to
go for a walk on the water.

Fred Trueman on Geoff Boycott's
move to Poole Harbour

During a Test match in the West Indies, Merv
Hughes didn't say a word to Viv Richards, but
continued to stare at him after deliveries.

Richards: This is my island, my
culture. Don't you be staring at
me. In my culture we just bowl.

Merv didn't reply, but after he dismissed
him he announced to the batsman:

In my culture we just say fuck off.

CRICKETERS ON CRICKETERS

Geoffrey is the only fellow I've met who fell in love with himself at a young age and has remained faithful ever since.

Dennis Lillee on Geoff Boycott

I remember the first time I walked into the Lancashire dressing room, when I was 16, all these guys – Atherton, Fairbrother, Akram – you just drop your shopping, you don't know where to put yourself. With Botham, I could barely pick my shopping up.

Andrew Flintoff, English cricketer, on the first time he met Ian Botham

A natural mistimer of the ball.

Angus Fraser on Michael Atherton

I don't know what these fellows are doing, but whatever they are doing, they sure are doing it well.

Pete Sampras, American tennis player, on watching Lara and Ambrose at Lord's

If it had been a cheese roll, it
would never have got past him.

Graham Gooch, former England cricket
captain, on Mike Gatting being bowled
out in the 1993 Old Trafford Test

I don't suppose I can call you a
lucky bleeder when you've got 347.

Angus Fraser, former English cricketer, to Brian Lara

Off the field, he could be your
lifelong buddy, but out in the middle,
he had all the loveable qualities
of a demented rhinoceros.

Colin McCool, Australian cricketer
(1916–1986), on Bill O'Reilly

One of the few men capable
of looking more dishevelled at
the start of a six-hour century
than at the end of it.

Martin Johnson, English cricket journalist,
on Michael Atherton after his century at
Edgbaston against South Africa in 1998

Eeyore without the joie de vivre.

Mike Selvey on Angus Fraser

Hogg suggested we survey
the back of the Adelaide
Oval, and I don't think he had
a tennis match on his mind.

Graham Yallop, former Australian cricketer, on a
difference of opinion with his teammate Rodney Hogg

If there were 22 Trevor Baileys
playing in a match, who would
ever go and watch it?

Arthur Morris, former Australian cricketer

His game embraced a contempt
for his fate, a foaming fury
because to him, cricket was
a game of kill or be killed.

Peter Roebuck, English journalist, commentator
and former cricketer, on Viv Richards

CRICKETERS
V
THE PRESS

If there is a game
that attracts the half-
baked theorists more
than cricket, I have
yet to hear of it.

Fred Trueman

Cricket is full of theorists who can ruin your game in no time.

Ian Botham

———

They smile and then they stab.

Geoff Boycott

———

Generally, the people out on the pitch are the ones who know how to play the game, not the ones who are writing about it.

Marcus Trescothick, English cricketer

Mark Waugh's a great friend of mine and he's got to make a few quid somehow, even by joining you blokes.

Shane Warne, speaking to the press

If I had my time over again, I would never have played cricket. Why? Because of people like you. The press do nothing but criticise.

Garry Sobers, former West Indian cricketer

I will never be accepted by the snob press.

Raymond Illingworth, English cricket commentator and former cricketer

I have grown to trust and like several of the cricket writers. Equally, there are some I trust, but don't like, others I like, but don't trust and the occasional individual I neither like nor trust.

Bob Willis, *The Captain's Diary*

The media make mountains from molehills to satisfy producers and editors alike.

Mark Nicholas, English commentator and former cricketer

Newspapers are only good enough for wrapping up fish and chips.

Martin Crowe, former New Zealand batsman

You buggers have been lampooning
me and harpooning me.

**Ted Dexter, former English cricketer,
to assembled media**

They find a ghost in everything.

**Shakoor Rana, Pakistani umpire,
on the English tabloids**

Will someone remove this buffoon?

**Michael Atherton, frustrated with the broken English
of Asghar Ali of the Pakistani Press Association**

You have to try to reply to criticism
with your intellect, not your ego.

Mike Brearley on handling the media

British Airways steward: Would you like me
to take anything home for you?
Bob Willis, England captain: Yes, 34
journalists and two camera crews.

England's tour of the West Indies, 1986

ENGLISH CRICKET

Cricket has been played pretty solidly in this country, and indeed throughout the Empire ever since the Norman Conquest, except perhaps during the Dark Ages, when bad light stopped play.

Ralph Wotherspoon and L. N. Jackson, *Some Sports and Pastimes of the English,* 1937

English cricket, once a byword for order and efficiency, with sporadic exhibitions of genius, is today – as Sir Denis Thatcher might crisply put it – about as much use as a one-legged man at an arse-kicking party.

Profile of the England cricket team, *The Sunday Times*

I can't bat, can't bowl and can't field these days. I've every chance of being picked for England.

Ray East, former English cricketer

If they want me to get down to 12 stone, I would have to cut off a leg.

Ian Blackwell, 17-stone English all-rounder, on the England selectors' orders for him to lose weight

You can't have 11 Darren Goughs in your side – it would drive you nuts. It would be like having 11 Phil Tufnells.

Darren Gough on the future of
England's bowling attack

Many Continentals think life is a game; the English think cricket is a game.

George Mikes, Hungarian-born
British author (1912–1987)

Our cricket is too gentle – all of it.

Alec Stewart, former English cricketer
and England captain

In an England cricket 11, the flesh may be of the south, but the bone is of the north and the backbone is Yorkshire.

Sir Leonard Hutton

It has been said of the unseen army of the dead, on their everlasting march, that when they are passing a rural cricket ground, the Englishmen fall out of the ranks for a moment to lean over a gate and smile.

J. M. Barrie

John Henry Newman was as English as roast beef, even if he lacked a passion for cricket.

Clifford Longley, English journalist

Is there no way in which Richards of Hampshire could be co-opted into the English Test side? Can no patriotic English girl be persuaded to marry him? He is quite personable... Failing that, could not some elderly gentleman adopt him?

The Times

Bloody medieval most of them.

Ian Botham on the English cricket administration

England will win if Camilla Parker bowls.

Australian fans' banner

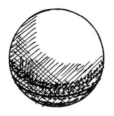

During the ICC Trophy many of the teams conversed on the field in foreign tongues with the odd cricket phrase coming through in English. One such side was Israel – a really happy band of village standard players – from whose chatter I suddenly picked up the term 'in-swinger'. On asking their Jewish captain as to why he had no translation for this type of delivery, he informed me that this was because nobody had bowled in the Old Testament.

Gordon Hewitt, journalist, 'The Good, The Bad and The Ridiculous', *The Cricketer*

Where the English language
is unspoken there can
be no real cricket.

Neville Cardus

There have always been many
cricket cultures and those who
try and narrow it down to one,
who always claim to be the
defenders of some inner purity,
are the enemies of the game.

Mike Marqusee, American writer

ENGLAND
V
AUSTRALIA

In Affectionate
Remembrance of
ENGLISH CRICKET,
which died at the Oval on
29th AUGUST, 1882,
Deeply lamented by a large
circle of sorrowing friends
and acquaintances. RIP
NB – The body will be
cremated and the ashes
taken to Australia.

Satirical obituary published in *The Sporting Times*,
1882, following England's defeat to Australia. The
English media then dubbed the next English tour
to Australia as 'the quest to regain The Ashes' and
the tournament as it is known today was born

The aim of English Test cricket is, in fact, mainly to beat Australia.

Jim Laker, English cricketer (1922–1986)

Maybe it's the tally-ho attitude. You know, there'll always be an England, all that Empire crap they dish out. But I never could cop the Poms.

Jeff Thompson

Australian fans will have gone to bed at three in the morning knowing the sun will still come up in the morning, but you don't like losing to England at anything.

Geoff Lawson, Australian journalist and former cricketer

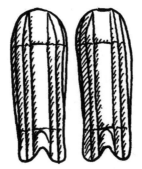

If the Poms bat first, let's
tell the taxi to wait.

Australian fans' banner

You know you're in Melbourne
when you're walking through the
park and you see someone kicking
the footy with cricket pads on.

Hung Le, Australian comedian

FASTBALLS:
QUICK QUIPS

I'd have looked even
faster in colour.

Fred Trueman

I've done the elephant. I've done the poverty. I might as well go home.

Phil Tufnell, during England's tour of India

———•———

A dry fart!

Phil Edmonds, former English cricketer, on being asked what he looked forward to most upon returning from a long tour of India

———•———

I just want to get into the middle and get the right sort of runs.

Robin Smith, South African cricketer, on suffering from diarrhoea on tour in India

David Gower: Do you want
Gatting a foot wider?
Chris Cowdrey: No. He'd burst.

During the 1985 India v England Test in Calcutta

Ken Barrington: Let's cut out
some of the quick singles.
Fred Titmus: OK! We'll cut
out yours, Ken.

During a mid-wicket conference in a Test match

Merv Hughes and Javed Miandad in the 1991
Adelaide Test against Pakistan. Hughes was less
than impressed when Javed called him a 'fat bus
conductor' as the pair squared up to one another.
A few balls later, Hughes got his man and as
Javed walked past, could not resist shouting:

Tickets, please!

Merv Hughes.

Steve Waugh, former Australian cricketer, on
being asked what his favourite animal was

Dustin Hoffman and some Aussie bowlers in the act of appealing.

Darryl Cullinan, on being asked who
his favourite actors were

It can't have been Gatt. Anything he takes up to his room after nine o'clock, he eats.

Ian Botham commenting on Mike Gatting and the 'barmaid affair'

GOOD DAYS AND BAD

If my grandfather was
alive, he would have
slaughtered a cow.

Makhaya Ntini, South African cricketer,
after taking five for 75 in the second
Test against England at Lord's

Yesterday at The Oval had
to be the most thrilling moment
of my life... perhaps after
the birth of my children.

**Gladstone Small, former English cricketer,
on the England Ashes win of 2005**

—◆—

I can't really say I'm batting
badly. I'm not batting long
enough to be batting badly.

Greg Chappell, former Australian cricketer

—◆—

You should play every game as if it's
your last, but make sure you perform
well enough to ensure that it's not.

John Emburey, former English cricketer

It's a bit like the four-minute
mile or climbing Mount Everest.
Someone is going to do it
eventually, but no one forgets
the person who did it first.

**Sir Richard Hadlee, former New Zealand cricketer,
on being first to score 400 Test wickets**

In real cricket, the player who has
developed imagination and skill
makes the game, but in the one-day
match it is the other way around.
The match dictates to the player.

Brian Close

The game you are frightened
of losing is not worth winning.

**Benny Green, British jazz saxophonist
and writer (1927–1998)**

I'm very concerned for our middle order. We've already called on the immediate next people down, so who do you go to next? I've got a four-year-old son who might like a go.

Ken Rutherford, former New Zealand cricketer, after a big defeat by Australia in 1993

The way to do it is enjoy your cricket and relax, to accept occasionally you'll have a bad day and try to get out of bed with a smile on your face.

Graeme Thorpe, English cricketer

I always played to win.

Hansie Cronje, South African cricketer (1969–2002)

I play best when I'm surrounded
by people who appreciate me.

Geoff Boycott

Any time the West Indies lose, I cry.

Lance Gibbs, former West Indian batsman

Bowl better and bat better.

Ricky Ponting, Australian cricketer, on how
Australia can improve their performance

Only two problems with our team. Brewer's droop and financial cramp. Apart from that we ain't bloody good enough.

Charlie Parker, English cricketer (1882–1959)

You are only as good as your last game.

Ian Botham

I think we are all slightly down
in the dumps after another loss.
We may be in the wrong sign...
Venus may be in the wrong
juxtaposition with somewhere else.

Ted Dexter explaining away England's seventh
successive Test loss to Australia at Lord's, 1993

Nobody's perfect. You know
what happened to the last man
who was – they crucified him.

Geoff Boycott

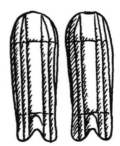

IS THAT WHAT THEY MEANT TO SAY?

I've seen batting all over the world. And in other countries, too.

Keith Miller, Australian cricketer (1919–2004)

It's tough for a natural
hooker to give it up.

Ian Chappell, former Australian batsman

❧

I condone anyone who
tampers with the ball.

Allan Lamb, South African-born English cricketer,
who may just have meant 'condemn'

❧

Anyone foolish enough to predict
the outcome of this match is a fool.

Fred Trueman

The bowler's Holding,
the batsman's Willey.

Brian Johnston

———•———

Unless something happens
that we can't predict, I don't
think a lot will happen.

Fred Trueman

———•———

There were congratulations
and high sixes all round.

Richie Benaud

On the first day, Logie decided
to chance his arm and it came off.

Trevor Bailey, former English cricketer

❧

Strangely, in slow-motion
replay, the ball seemed to hang
in the air for even longer.

David Acfield, English cricketer

❧

Against Surrey, tomorrow,
Somerset will beat Middlesex.

Lloyd's Weekly

Reporter: Do you feel that the selectors and yourself have been vindicated by the result?

Gatting: I don't think the press are vindictive. They can write what they want.

Mike Gatting, former English cricketer

THE JOYS OF CRICKET

Watching cricket
has given me more
happiness than any
other activity in which I
have engaged. Lord's
on a warm day, with
a bottle, a mixed bag
of sandwiches, and a
couple of spare tyres
in a despatch case,
and I don't care who
is playing whom.

A. A. Milne, English author (1882–1956)

There is no talk, none so witty and brilliant, that is so good as cricket talk, when memory sharpens memory, and the dead live again – the regretted, the forgotten – and the old happy days of burned out Junes revive.

Andrew Lang, Scottish poet and novelist (1844–1912)

❦

Cricket is indescribable. How do you describe an orgasm?

Greg Matthews, former Australian cricketer

❦

To go to a cricket match for nothing but cricket is as though a man were to go into an inn for nothing but drink.

Neville Cardus

The love of cricket nowadays seems to be confined to those who watch it or read about it.

Arthur Mailey, Australian cricketer (1886–1967)

But after all, it's not the winning that matters, is it? Or is it? It's – to coin a word – the amenities that count: the smell of the dandelions, the puff of the pipe, the click of the bat, the rain on the neck, the chill down the spine, the slow, exquisite coming on of sunset and dinner and rheumatism.

Alastair Cooke, English-born American journalist and broadcaster (1908–2004)

In my opinion cricket is too great a game to think about statistically.

E. H. Hendren, English cricketer (1889–1962)

If I knew I was going
to die today, I'd still
want to hear the
cricket scores.

J. H. Hardy

LADIES AND CRICKET

We have nothing
against man cricketers.
Some of them are
quite nice people, even
though they don't win
as often as we do.

Rachael Hayhoe-Flint

When we were living in Sydney a friend told me that one night, while she and her husband were making love, she suddenly noticed something sticking in his ear. When she asked him what it was he replied, 'Be quiet! I'm listening to the cricket.'

Vicky Rantzen, journalist, *The Observer*

———————

A loving wife is better than making 50 in cricket, or even 99, beyond that I will not go.

J. M. Barrie

———————

Women are for batsmen, beer is for bowlers. God help the all-rounders.

Fred Trueman

Ladies playing cricket – absurd.
Just like a man trying to knit.

Sir Leonard Hutton

❧—•—❧

Oh God! If there be cricket in
heaven let there also be rain.

**Lord Alec Douglas-Home, politician (1903–
1995), *Prayer of a Cricketer's Wife***

❧—•—❧

How can the ladies hurt their
delicate fingers, and even bring them
to blisters, with holding a nasty filthy
bat? How can their sweet delicate
fingers bear the jarrings attending
the catching of a dirty ball?

**The 3rd Duke of Dorset in response to the
proposition that women be allowed to play
cricket, *Ladies & Gentlemen's Magazine***

The MCC should change
their name to the MCP.

Diana Edulji, Indian women's captain, calling
the MCC male chauvinist pigs after being
refused entry to the Lord's pavilion

Popular opinion would be wrong
if it ever thought that the M in
MCC could stand for misogyny.
Quite the reverse is the case. But
it may well be that in this changing
world there would be one small
part of London which affords
refuge for the hunted male animal.

Jack Bailey, former English cricketer
and MCC secretary

The days of women's
cricket being seen
as a knicker parade
must be over.

**Norma Izard, former England manager and
one of the first female members of MCC**

Women find it more than difficult
not to cross and uncross
their legs under his gaze.

Lord Tim Hudson, English eccentric,
on the sex appeal of Ian Botham

The authorities should consider
that a cricketer is more likely to
have a proper night's sleep with his
wife in bed beside him, rather than
a temporary stand-in and all the
parallel gymnastics that would follow.

Lindsay Lamb

Pitches are like wives – you can never tell how they're going to turn out.

Sir Leonard Hutton

My friend Imran Khan, who is a famous cricketer and a very popular man with the ladies, has bodyguards outside his room, warding women off. I have guys warding them in.

Zia Mahmood, Pakistani bridge player

LITERARY CRICKET

Football offers
the world clichés;
rugby produces
facial deformity;
hockey provides
an acceptable
outlet for psychotic
violence; cricket
alone breeds myths.

Unknown

Baseball and cricket are beautiful
and highly stylised medieval war
substitutes, chess made flesh,
a mixture of proud chivalry and
base – in both senses – greed.

John Fowles, English novelist and
essayist (1926–2005)

I don't think I can be expected
to take seriously a game which
takes less than three days
to reach its conclusion.

Tom Stoppard, Czechoslovakian-born English
playwright, rejecting baseball in favour of cricket

It's not in support of cricket but as
an earnest protest against golf.

Max Beerbohm, English critic, essayist and
caricaturist (1872–1956), when asked to
contribute to W. G. Grace's testimonial

Strolling about the theatre one evening, he said on seeing me, 'Oh! Hicks, do you play cricket?' I said, 'Yes I do, Mr Barrie.' 'Well, will you come down to Sandwich and play against the fire brigade men for me?' he enquired. I said I should be delighted, but it would be impossible as I should be unable to get back to London in time to act that night. 'Oh, don't bother about that,' said Barrie, 'we can put on the understudy.'

Sir Seymour Hicks, English actor, recalling the time he played the part of Andrew McPhail, the medical student, in J. M. Barrie's play *Walker London* at Toole's Theatre in 1892, *Sunday Express*

Sir Donald Bradman
Would have been a very glad man
If his Test average had
been .06 more
Than 99.94

T. N. E. Smith

As in life so in death lies
a bat of renown,
Slain by a lorry (three ton);
His innings is over, his
bat is laid down;
To the end a poor judge of a run.

Inscription on an English gravestone

Cricket is full of glorious
chances, and the Goddess who
presides over it loves to bring
down the most skilful player.

Thomas Hughes

I see them in foul dug-
outs, gnawed by rats,
And lying in the
ruined temples,
lashed by rain,
Dreaming of
things they did with
balls and bats.

Siegfried Sassoon, English soldier and poet
(1886–1967), who lived as a country gentleman,
hunting and playing cricket, before being sent to
fight in the First World War, 'The Dreamers'

You know Lord's? Well, once I played there
And a ball I hit to leg
Struck the umpire's head, stayed there
As a nest retains an egg.

Harry Graham, English poet (1874–
1936), *Ruthless Rhymes*

Looking backward we could almost
see, suspended with the most
delicate equipoise above the flat
little island, the ghostly shapes of
those twin orbs of the Empire, the
cricket ball and the black ball.

Patrick Leigh Fermor, English author,
scholar and former soldier

To expect a personality to survive
the disintegration of the brain is like
expecting a cricket club to survive
when all of its members are dead.

Bertrand Russell, Welsh writer, logician,
philosopher and mathematician (1872–1970)

We didn't have any metaphors in my
day. We didn't beat about the bush.

Fred Trueman

Thy fame has spread
whatever bat and ball
Ring with their joyous
clatter o'er the field
On this thy birthday
may no shadow fall
And may it still a
further hundred yield;
Thou art the centre
of a million eyes
Who love one summer
game and sunny skies.

'To W. G. Grace', to commemorate his jubilee, 1898

There's a breathless hush
in the Close tonight –
Ten to make and a match to win –
A bumping pitch and a blinding light,
An hour to play and the last man in.
And it's not for the sake
of a ribboned coat,
Or the selfish hope of
a season's fame,
But his Captain's hand on
his shoulder smote –
'Play up! play up! and play the game!'

Sir Henry Newbolt, English author and
poet (1862–1938), 'Vitaë Lampada'

We have played Eton and were
most confoundedly beat, however
it was some comfort to me that
I got 11 notches in the first
innings and seven the second...

Lord Byron, Anglo-Scottish poet (1788–1824), in a
letter referring to the initial match in a series in 1805.
Byron's actual scores were somewhat different

I tend to believe that cricket is the greatest thing that God ever created on earth... certainly greater than sex, although sex isn't too bad either.

Harold Pinter, English playwright and theatre director

Alas, I don't even know enough about cricket to attack it. Anyway, I wouldn't attack it as I much prefer it to muddied oafs.

Graham Greene, English writer and novelist (1904–1991)

Capital gain – smart sport – fine exercise – very.

Charles Dickens, English writer (1812–1870), on cricket, *The Pickwick Papers*

That Bill's a foolish fellow;
He has given me a black eye.
He does not know how
to handle a bat
Any more than a dog, or a cat;
He has knock'd down the wicket,
And broken his stumps
And runs without shoes
to save his pumps.

William Blake, English poet (1757–
1827), 'The Song of Tilly Lally'

While batting once, the Prince
of Wales – whose name
was Frederick Louis,
Was hit upon the head, and so
his legs went soft and gooey.
He later died because he got
that bouncer to the brain,
So in this case you might say
the result was 'play stopped reign'.

Richard Stilgoe, English lyricist and
musician, 'The Prince of Wales'

MISUNDERSTANDING CRICKET

Sometimes, people think it's like polo, played on horseback, and I remember one guy thought it was a game involving insects.

Clayton Lambert, West Indian cricketer, explaining cricket to Americans

Basically it's just a whole bunch
of blokes standing around
scratching themselves.

Kathy Lette, Australian author

It's a silly game that nobody wins.

Thomas Fuller, English clergyman
and historian (1608–1661)

Generally regarded as
an incomprehensibly dull
and pointless game.

Douglas Adams, English radio dramatist and author
(1952–2001), *Life, the Universe and Everything*

It is not true that the English
invented cricket as a way of making
all other human endeavours look
interesting and lively; that was
merely an unintended side effect.
I don't wish to denigrate a sport
that is enjoyed by millions, some
of them awake and facing the
right way, but it is an odd game.

Bill Bryson, American author, *Down Under*

I would rather watch a man at his toilet than on a cricket field.

Robert Morley, English actor (1908–1992)

Baseball has the great advantage over cricket of being ended sooner.

George Bernard Shaw, Irish literary critic, playwright and essayist (1856–1950)

Cricket? It's rubbish. I don't like it. It's not a very emotive game.

Juninho, Brazilian footballer

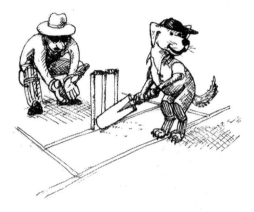

A cricketer – a creature very
nearly as stupid as a dog.

Bernard Levin, English journalist, author and
broadcaster (1928–2004), *The Times*

After years of patient study
(and with cricket there can be no
other kind), I have decided that
there is nothing wrong with the
game that the introduction of golf
carts wouldn't fix in a hurry.

Bill Bryson, *Down Under*

Of course it's frightfully dull! That's the whole point!... To go to cricket to be thrilled is as stupid as to go to a Chekhov play in search of melodrama.

Robert Morley, *The Final Test*

THE NATURE OF
THE GAME

Personally, I have
always looked
on cricket as
organised loafing.

William Temple, Ninth Archbishop
of Canterbury (1881–1944)

Distrusting the arts, the English found a substitute in cricket – a timeless blend of formal dancing, rhetoric and comic opera.

Kenneth Gregory, *Cricket's Last Romantic*

There is no more amateurish professional game in the world than cricket.

John Emburey

Cricket is the easiest sport in the world to take over. Nobody bothered to pay the players what they were worth.

Kerry Packer, Australian publishing, media and gaming tycoon (1937–2005), commenting on the foundation of World Series Cricket

Cricket is certainly a very good
and wholesome exercise, yet it may
be abused if either great or little
people make it their business.

Gentleman's Magazine

As a substitute for music, I watch
ballet; the dance, for me, is music
made visible. Cricket I watch for
almost the same reason, except that
its music, so to speak, is abstract...
I see the game as ceremony.

David Wright, *A Deaf Man Looks at Cricket*

Cricket is the only game I can
enjoy without taking sides.

A. A. Milne

Cricket's a game, not a competition.

George Hirst, English cricketer (1871–1954)

I'm not interested in sport. I'm
interested in cricket. I'm always
surprised to find cricket books
in the library in the sports
section, next to football.

John Minnion, English illustrator and captain
of the *New Statesman* cricket side

We don't play this game for fun.

Wilfred Rhodes, English cricketer (1877–1973)

A Test match is like a painting.
A one-day match is like a
Rolf Harris painting.

Ian Chappell

———❖———

One-day cricket is like fast
food. No one wants to cook.

Viv Richards, former West Indian cricketer

———❖———

One-day cricket is an exhibition.
Test cricket is an examination.

Henry Blofeld

I've heard it said that this game
at Test level is 50 per cent
in the mind, 50 per cent in the
heart, and bugger technique,
and that's not far off the mark.

Raymond Illingworth

Cricket is battle and service
and sport and art.

Douglas Jardine, English cricketer (1900–1958)

OFF THE PITCH

I have been to many
functions where some
great cricketers of
the past have been
present. To see some
of them sink their
drink is to witness
performances as awe-
inspiring as ever any
of them displayed
on the cricket field.

Ian Botham

If I'd done a quarter of the things
of which I'm accused, I'd be pickled
in alcohol. I'd be a registered
drug addict and would have sired
half the children in the world's
cricket-playing countries.

Ian Botham

When you have to spend the tour
in your hotel room so you're not
stitched up, there's something wrong.

Ian Botham, England tour of the West Indies, 1986

Please don't make me
out to be a cad.

Mark Nicholas, speaking to the press after
revelations about his private life

I'd rather face Dennis Lillee
with a stick of rhubarb than
go through all that again.

**Ian Botham, cleared of assault charges
at Grimsby Crown Court**

If it is embarrassing then it is wrong, but if it is private, and hopefully delightful, then what could be better – even in the middle of a Test Match?

Ted Dexter on players' nocturnal activities in the wake of the Gatting 'barmaid affair'

THE PLAYERS

It is strange, but I think true, that all the time, day and night, somewhere in the world somebody is talking about Bradman.

Jack Ingham, Australian thoroughbred horse-breeder and racing enthusiast (1928–2003)

Surely Mr Adlard achieves a masterpiece of meiosis in saying that Gilbert Jessop 'should be included among the mighty hitters'? It is like saying that St. Peter's must find a place among the big churches of the world.

Laurence Meynell, English author (1899–1989)

The first rock and roll cricketer.

Sir Leonard Hutton on Ian Botham

Difficult to be more laid back without being actually comatose.

Frances Edmonds, English author and broadcaster, on David Gower, *Daily Express*

It's like watching a swan. What you see on the surface bears no relation to the activity going on underneath.

David Gower on being accused of being too laid back

[He's got a] reputation for being awkward and arrogant, probably because he is awkward and arrogant.

Frances Edmonds on her husband, Phil

Charles Wright was the Captain of Notts, and had also got a century in the University match. He was a most delightful person, but by no means the complete *Encyclopaedia Britannica*.

The Cricketer

Easy to watch, difficult to
bowl to, and impossible to write
about. When you bowled to him
there weren't enough fielders;
when you wrote about him
there weren't enough words.

Cricket Prints, referring to Frank Woolley

If someone wore a chocolate bar on
his head, Goughie would follow suit.

Steve Oldham, former English
cricketer, on Darren Gough

The petty things of cricketing life
seem to be below Worrell. The
will to win at all costs is somehow
distasteful to him. The game,
not the result, means more.

Ron Roberts, Australian cricketer
(1928–2003), on Sir Frank Worrell

Others scored faster; hit the ball harder; more obviously murdered bowling. No one else, though, ever batted with such consummate skill.

John Arlott, English sports commentator
(1914–1991), on Jack Hobbs

Denis Compton was the only player to call his partner for a run and wish him good luck at the same time.

John Warr, former English cricketer

When we were children we asked my Uncle Charles what it was like to play cricket with W. G. Grace. 'The dirtiest neck I ever kept wicket behind,' was his crisp reply.

Lord Chandos

His personality was such that
it is remembered by those who
played with him to the exclusion
of his actual performance.

John Arlott on W. G. Grace

Had Grace been born in
ancient Greece *The Iliad* would
have been a different book.

The Bishop of Hereford, quoted by Clifford Bax
in *W. G. Grace, (Cricketing Lives* series)

POLITICIANS ON CRICKET

You do well to love cricket, because it is more free from anything sordid, anything dishonourable than any game in the world. To play it keenly, generously, self-sacrificingly is a moral lesson in itself, and the classroom is God's air and sunshine. Foster it, my brothers, so that it may attract all who find the time to play it, protect it from anything that will sully it, so that it may grow in favour with all men.

Lord Harris, Trindad-born English politician
and former England captain (1851–1932)

Cricket civilises people and creates good gentlemen. I want everyone to play cricket in Zimbabwe; I want ours to be a nation of gentlemen.

Robert Mugabe, executive president of Zimbabwe

Cricket can be a bridge and a glue... Cricket for peace is my mission.

Muhammad Zia-ul-Haq, former president of Pakistan (1924–1988)

Australians will always fight for these 22 yards. Lord's and its traditions belong to Australia just as much as to England.

John Curtin, Australian prime minister, in a speech to Lord's (1885–1945)

Mrs Thatcher is in the position of a Martian trying to understand cricket.

Neil Kinnock, Welsh politician, referring to the then prime minister's attitude towards football identity cards and the Taylor enquiry

Any cricketer would want to bowl to Bradman even if he were to hit them for six. It's the same with Robin.

Brian Walden, English journalist and former MP, on Robin Day and the politicians queuing to be lashed by his tongue

Explaining the rules of cricket is an excellent test for high-powered brains.

John Major, former British prime minister

Politics governs everything we do – the games we play, the way we play them, who we play.

John Arlott

Cricket had plunged me into politics long before I was aware of it. When I did turn to politics I did not have too much to learn.

C. L. R. James, Trinidad-born cricket journalist and author (1901–1989)

Say that cricket has nothing to do with politics and you say that cricket has nothing to do with life.

John Arlott

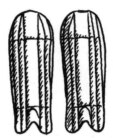

THE PRESENTATION
OF THE PLAYERS

It requires one
to assume such
indecent postures.

Oscar Wilde, Irish playwright, novelist
and poet (1854–1900)

Although we have all on occasion enjoyed proper muscular exercise, yet we strongly reprobate that of cricket, which is in all respects too violent, and, from the positions into which players must necessarily throw themselves, cannot fail to be productive of frequent injury to the body. Indeed... from the awkward posture occasioned by employing both arms at the same time in striking a distant object.

Dr Willich, *Domestic Encyclopaedia*

If you can't always play like a cricketer, you can at least look like one.

Sir Donald Bradman

I doubt if many of my contemporaries, especially the older ones, did many exercises. I have often tried to picture [Godfrey] Evans and [Denis] Compton doing press-ups in the outfield before the day's play, but so far have failed miserably.

Peter May, English cricketer (1929–1994)

If you like a white sun hat, always carry one with you. C. B. Fry played some of his greatest innings in a sun hat.

'Cross-Arrow', *The Cricketer*

Maybe I should smile a bit more...
raise the profile and have a nice
spin-off contract for wearing
something or other. But that's
not me. I look like I do on the field
because what I do is knackering.

Angus Fraser

Cricket needs umpires who
grace the general scene with
sartorial sharpness, instead of
resembling a pair of Balkan
refugees clad by Oxfam.

John Sheppard, former West Indian
cricketer, *The Cricketer*

The gum-chewing habit is very catching, and you will sometimes see a whole fielding team resembling a herd of cows at pasture.

R. C. Robertson-Glasgow, English cricketer
(1901–1965), *Crusoe on Cricket*

Chris Lewis baldly went where no other cricketer has gone before – and the prat without a hat spent two days in bed with sunstroke.

Unknown

THE PRESS STEP UP
TO THE CREASE

A second boundary, taken off the hip by a shaky batsman [Hick], had roughly the effect on Ambrose that the sight of alcohol seems to have on ayatollahs.

Peter Roebuck, *The Sunday Times*

Cricket must be the only business where you can make more money on one day than three.

Pat Gibson, Irish-born leading British quiz player, *Daily Express*

———•———

Bill Hudson lost 100 schooners of beer when he bet that Kevin Douglas Walters could not make 100 first time out against the Poms. Only when you have seen him bat and tested his self-possession do you realise how rash that wager really was.

Ian Wooldridge, English sports journalist, *The Cricketer*

———•———

It was like seeing the future and realising that it worked.

Steve Brenkley, English journalist, on Ben Hollioake, *The Independent on Sunday*

[Gower wore] an expression
of permanent pained
bewilderment, like a man who's
just stepped into a lift-shaft.

Michael Henderson, English journalist, on David
Gower in Derby v Leicester, *The Guardian*

[Courtney Walsh], who has
effectively lost West Indies both
their matches, was presented with
a carpet for not running out Salim
Jaffer off the final ball. He was
last seen trying to fly home on it.

Martin Johnson, *The Independent*

It was not unlike watching Lazarus rise from the dead and get mown down by a runaway truck on his way to meet his mates in the bar.

Ian Wooldridge on New Zealand's performance versus Pakistan in the 1992 World Cup, *Daily Mail*

It was perhaps inevitable that your God-given talent should be envied by those who sweat in shell-suits to achieve less dazzling results. But who would have believed that spite and stupidity could have so hijacked the glorious game? Corinth, it seems, has given way to Chelmsford and we are all the poorer for it.

Frances Edmonds on David Gower, *The Independent*

At least we are safe from an intoxicated rendition of 'There's only one Graeme Hick'. There are, quite clearly, two of them. The first one turns out for teams like Worcestershire and New Zealand's Northern Districts and plays like a god. The second one pulls on an England cap and plays like the anagram of a god.

Martin Johnson, *The Independent*

Here was English cricket's Messiah, preceded by Ian Botham's shaggy John the Baptist. Perhaps we should all have noticed that Hick became eligible to play for England on April Fool's day.

John Dugdale, English journalist, on Graeme Hick, *The Sunday Times*

Alan Green, the occasional
off-spinner, might just turn a
spin-drier but not much else.

**Mihir Bose, Indian journalist and
author, *The Sunday Times***

Cricket on pitches like this bears
the same relationship to the true
first-class cricket that target
shooting bears to Russian roulette.

**Malcolm Winter, on Northants v West Indies
at Northampton, *The Sunday Times***

Barring injuries or sexual
indiscretions between now
and next Thursday, the three
other newcomers [*Barnett,
Russell and Lawrence*] seem
certain to get the benefit of the
Peter May Emporium's giant
1988 England Cap Sale.

Matthew Engel, English journalist, *The Guardian*

Watching Clinton steal a match
in which Hick and Botham
are playing is like going to a
Pavarotti concert and seeing him
upstaged by Des O'Connor.

Mike Selvey, *The Guardian*

[Ted Dexter], the most charismatic cricketer of his generation, who used to roar thro' the Lord's gates on a 1,000cc motor-bike, will phut-phut his way back out of them on a metaphorical moped, his public persona having altered – in the space of four and a half years – from a latter day Lawrence of Arabia into something closer to Mr Magoo.

Martin Johnson, *The Independent*

[Ilott] is out of this game with a groin strain and thus joins Darren Gough, Chris Lewis and Andrew Caddick on the list of those more in line for a trip to Lourdes rather than Lord's.

Martin Johnson, *The Independent*

By close of play on Tuesday, having been set a target to win of just 194, England were 40 for eight off 14.5 overs. It was a collapse even more humiliating than that of John Major over voting rights in Brussels. Next morning, England's remaining wickets were taken quicker than a stray fiver in the Portobello Road. There were by now enough ducks on the field to feed an average family for a fortnight...

Profile of the England cricket team, *The Sunday Times*

RETIREMENT

Endless cricket, like endless anything else, simply grinds you down.

Ted Dexter

So I joined a Barclays Bank graduate training scheme in 1991. People were amazed I could contemplate such a swap. I suppose it was like John Major running away from his circus background to be an accountant.

John Carr, former English cricketer, on his leaving Middlesex, as reported by Rob Steen, *The Independent*

Golf is a game to be played between cricket and death.

Colin Ingleby-McKenzie, English cricketer (1933–2006)

A bout of jaundice took the edge off my stamina once and for all and I realised then that human bodies are not like vintage motor cars. No amount of rebuilding and polishing has the same effect.

Ted Dexter

Ask me that again when you're all in Dhaka and I'm in Rome, watching Chelsea playing Lazio!

Alec Stewart, on being asked if
he would regret retiring

I've had about ten operations. I'm a bit like a battered old Escort. You might find one panel left that's an original.

Ian Botham

I won't miss bowling 20 overs
uphill into the wind.

Ian Botham

For many sportsmen, coming face
to face with irrefutable evidence
of their mortality is the moment
they dread above all others.

Ian Botham

SCHOOLBOY
CRICKET

Years lost in early
life are irrecoverable,
especially in cricket.

Les Ames, English batsman (1905–1990)

When Merv leaves school,
he is going to have to be very
good at football and cricket.

**Former Australian cricketer Merv Hughes'
fifth form geography report**

Mike said that he'd read
Wilbur Smith when he was
eight. That's why he went to
Cambridge and I didn't.

**Graeme Hick, Zimbabwean cricketer,
on his captain Michael Atherton**

He's Biggles, the VC, El Alamein,
the tank commander, he's everything.
I mean, how could a schoolboy
not want to be like Ian Botham?

Lord Tim Hudson

Sometimes an unlucky boy will drive his cricket ball full in my face.

Dr Samuel Johnson, English poet, essayist, biographer, lexicographer, and literary critic (1709–1784), *The Rambler*

I well remember... at my Big School, after I missed a catch at long-leg, saying to myself 'O Lord take away my life, for I am not worthy to live!'

John Cowper Powys, English-Welsh writer, lecturer, and philosopher (1872–1963), *Autobiography*

A boy running hell for leather at Winchester cannoned head down into E. R. Wilson on his way to school, looked up and in horror gasped 'Good God', to which E. R. Wilson gently replied, 'But strictly incognito.'

George Lyttelton, English politician and author (1709–1773)

What's the point in 'O' Levels?
They don't help you play cricket!

Ian Botham

—◆—

Brian Johnston's cheeky wit did not start
and end with cricket. While attending
Oxford, he was at a lecture on Henry V.

Professor: Now let us turn to
Henry's wife – Henrietta.

Johnston, from the back of the auditorium:
Did he really, sir?

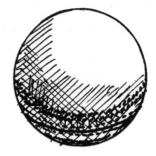

THE WEATHER AND
THE GROUNDS

The elements are
cricket's presiding
geniuses.

Neville Cardus

It is extremely cold here. The England fielders are keeping their hands in pockets between balls.

Christopher Martin-Jenkins, English cricket commentator and journalist

I enjoyed it, but if I go back again I'll wear a tin hat.

Laurie Lee, English poet and novelist (1914–1997), after being knocked unconscious by a flying beer bottle during a game between Australia and New Zealand

Four separate stoppages for rain and bad light left the day as shapeless as a Demis Roussos costume.

Glenn Moore, English journalist, on Kent v Middlesex at Canterbury in 1994, *The Independent*

Clearly the gods rule cricket...
A spot of rain, a flash of sun, a
swathe of wind, a flick of hail, a
yield of earth, a tuft of turf, an
errant mole, a humid noon, a pollen
surge – all or any of these natural
and uncontrollable forces of the
weather can be crucial. Cricket is
the rawest game left on the planet.

**Melvyn Bragg, English author and
broadcaster, *On the Boundary***

What is both surprising and
delightful is that spectators are
allowed and even expected to join in
the vocal part of the game... There
is no reason why the field should not
try to put the batsman off his stroke
at the critical moment by neatly timed
disparagements of his wife's fidelity
and his mother's respectability.

George Bernard Shaw

The advent of a mosque with its burnished copper dome has made navigation towards [Lord's] much easier for people coming from that direction [Regent's Park]. There was a brief period when the muezzin's amplified calls to prayer could be heard tantalisingly in the middle of the cricket pitch, but that all stopped after local inhabitants had secured an injunction against the romantic but distinctly alien sound.

Geoffrey Moorhouse, English author, *Lord's*

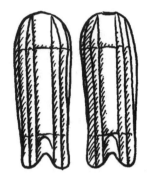

WICKET PHILOSOPHY

Ninety per cent of
cricket is played
in the mind.

Sir Richard Hadlee

All is vanity, but cricket.

Revd John Mitford, Editor of *Gentleman's Magazine* (1781–1851)

The English are not very spiritual people, so they invented cricket to give them some idea of eternity.

George Bernard Shaw

Cricket: A game invented by religious fundamentalists to explain the idea of eternal hell to non-Christian indigenous peoples of the former British Empire.

Joseph O'Connor, Irish novelist

What do they know of cricket
who only cricket know?

C. L. R. James

What is human life but
a game of cricket?

3rd Duke of Dorchester, *Ladies'
and Gentlemen's Magazine*

For when the One
Great Scorer comes
To write against
your name,
He marks not that
you won or lost
But how you
played the game.

Grantland Rice, American sports
journalist (1880–1954)

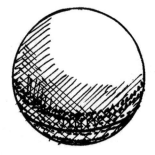

EXTRA INNINGS:
ODDBALLS

Remember, linseed
oil for your bat, olive
oil for your lamb.

Allan Lamb

Sir, Today I learned with interest that the average height of our current Test side is 6 feet. Since there are 11 playing members of the team their total length is therefore 66 feet or 22 yards – the length of the wicket. Is this significant?

Mrs Patricia Crozier, letter to *The Times*

Sir, I was horrified to learn the other day that there is now a cricket club in Finland. I left England 25 years ago to get away from people like yourself. Is nowhere sacred?

Letter to the editor of *The Helsinki Cricketer*

I would have died for Yorkshire. I suppose once or twice I nearly did.

Brian Close

I learned that there was a safe and far-away place on the field called 'deep' which I always chose. When 'over' was called, I simply went more and more 'deep' until I was sitting on the steps of the pavilions reading the plays of Noël Coward.

John Mortimore, former English cricketer

It's like Manchester United getting a penalty and Bryan Robson taking it with his head.

David Lloyd on the reverse sweep

I'll turn the phone off and just watch Ceefax around midday.

Graeme Swann, English cricketer, on not being called up to play in the 2005 Ashes squad

I don't think I've actually drunk a beer for 15 years, except a few Guinnesses in Dublin, where it's the law.

Ian Botham

Poisoned by his mother? It is good, very good. It ranks up there with 'I got it from the toilet seat'.

Dick Pound, chairman of the World Anti-Doping Agency, commenting on Australian spin bowler Shane Warne's explanation that he tested positive for a banned substance because he had taken a diuretic given to him by his mother

———

Many forget that W. G. Grace was a respected doctor besides being a cricketing legend. One day a timid man turned up at the surgery and asked, 'Is the doctor in?' 'Of course he's in,' snapped the assistant. 'He's been batting since Monday.'

Unknown

———

Let's be getting at them before they get at us.

W. G. Grace

I suppose going out on your first date is always more exciting than when you've been married for 20 years.

Adam Hollioake, former Australian cricketer who played for England, on the challenge of cricket for him towards the end of his career

❦

After the 1776 Revolution, the question of a name for the Chief Executive of the USA was discussed. It was suggested that the word President be used. John Adams thereupon remarked, 'There are Presidents of fire companies and cricket clubs.'

Stephen Green, 'Some Cricket Records', Archives, vol. XVIII, no. 80, 1988

Wouldn't it be better if
I got in the fridge?

Qasim Omar, former Pakistani batsman,
receiving ice-pack treatment for bruises
caused by Australian fast bowlers

He crossed the line between
eccentricity and idiocy far too often
for someone who was supposed
to be running English cricket.

Ian Botham on Ted Dexter

You can't consider yourself a
county cricketer until you've
eaten half a ton of lettuce.

Garry Sobers

Ask me for the biggest highlight
of my career when I'm lying on my
deathbed – then I'll tell you.

Ian Botham

What a magnificent
shot! No, he's out.

Tony Greig, South African-born
commentator and former cricketer